DUNLIN :

Lessons for an Apprentice Eel Catcher

Alex Toms

***

Lessons for an Apprentice Eel Catcher

Published by Dunlin Press in 2018

Dunlin Press
Wivenhoe, Essex
dunlinpress.com | @dunlinpress

A CIP record of this book is available from the British Library.

ISBN: 978-0-9931259-5-9

Set in Helvetica, Garamond Pro and Berthold Akzidenz Grotesk.
Printed in Great Britain by Lightning Source.
Cover illustration and design by Ella Johnston.

For Dominic and Sebastian

Contents

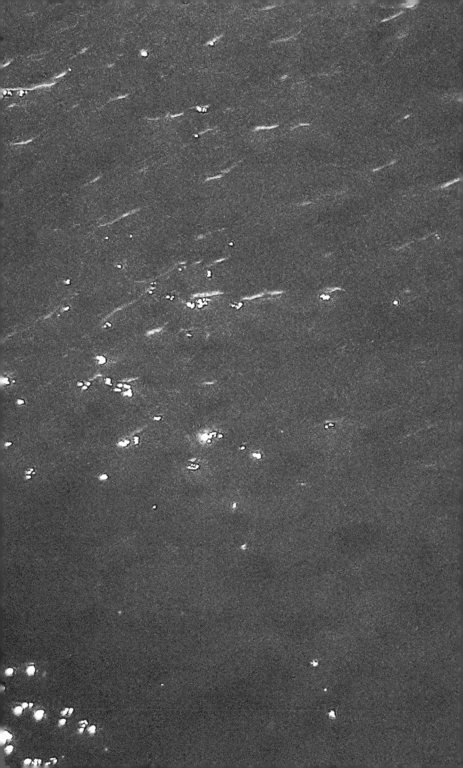

Lessons for an Apprentice Eel Catcher

Your day begins before the last stars have faded,
and the river still dreams
beneath its blanket of mist. It ends at sunset
when you've laid your last trap.

You will never be idle. When you're not
catching or selling, there are traps to weave
from willow strips. Blisters will pearl
your fingers – the only jewels you'll ever wear.

You'll be out in all weathers: when elvers of rain
trickle down your neck; when the sun beats down,
heavy as the hand of God. The elements
will burnish your skin, turn you into a living icon.

Like a monk's, your life will be one of toil
and solitude, but blessed with unexpected
glimpses of God: in the dazzle of a dragonfly;
in the whirling dervish dance of the eels.

This is your inheritance: the watery miles
our people have fished since before
the cathedral reared like a beast
in its scaffolding cage. Some gave their lives

so that we might know where weeds weave snares,
where the mud drags you down. You'll learn to respect
the fens, understand they're glad to give
their slippery gifts,

but swift to take too. Sometimes, when marsh warblers
chant their evensong, mist will swing towards you,
as though from a giant censer. It will wrap around you –
a cloak of icy eels, your prayers freezing in your throat.

Faint, winking lights will appear:
your ancestors, holding lanterns –
a string of glowing rosary beads
to guide you on your way.

The Postman and the Swans

No longer Michael the postman,
but Mikhail the farmer,
hauling sacks of feed instead of mail.

Spring brought him a girl; her Cyrillic
fell like flakes around him, melted on his tongue.
Twenty years on, his life is nearly complete,

but when Bewick's swans leave to winter
in England's mild and misty grey,
he thinks of his children,

their faces blurred,
like faces at a window
franked by English rain.

The Garden of Intelligence

After King Wen of Zhou

I have sent my armies to the furthest reaches
of my kingdom, to bring back animals

that will encourage the pursuit of knowledge.
So now I have a Garden of Intelligence,

spread before me like an unrolled scroll.
From the window in my private quarters,

I watch my concubines take dainty steps:
peahens dressed in peacock colours,

gowns trailing behind them like tailfeathers.
I have chosen creatures to symbolise

each of the elements: for earth –
Siberian tigers. They teach the merits of stealth

with their supple, weaving dance, which fools us into thinking
there are only shadows among the trees.

Golden carp show us how to be fluid in our thinking,
as they swerve beneath the surface, puzzling invisible mazes.

Air is represented by the wise crane,
whose wings write the evening sky

with sweeping strokes.
For the last, most fickle of elements,

the peacock – incarnation of the phoenix.
Fettered by their own beauty, they cannot fly far,

and when they do attempt flight,
it is a spectacle, almost ungainly.

This demonstrates the rewards of determination,
for in those shrieking seconds of weightlessness,

their tailfeathers light up the sky
like fireworks.

Becoming Sei

After Sei Shōnagon

i
In the heart of a palace
with hierarchies, traditions

more complex
than origami folds,

you spent your days
as a shadow flitting

behind curtains and paper screens,
hidden from men

except perhaps
for a glimpse of your arm,

smooth as a stamen
inside the flower of your sleeve,

unfurling to snatch
a hastily passed note

written on violet paper
tied to a wisteria sprig –

a butterfly to brighten
the blank ream of days.

ii
Your life is written in invisible ink
until the day

the Empress presents you with
a bundle of paper,

bids you write something
to rival the work of the scholars

in the Emperor's Court.
That night you dream of your favourite robe

hanging on its scenting frame. You pull a loose thread,
stare amazed

as mountains, birds, rivers, flowers
free themselves,

silver silk snaking through the air.
It hovers over the paper

before spilling like a waterfall,
turning to ink on contact.

iii
Kneeling at your desk,
grinding your ink stick,

you work your stories free.
Characters from Court

become characters on the page.
You take your place among them,

no longer invisible,
but slowly coming into focus,

your existence affirmed
by slick black ink.

You watch it seep
into the page's fibres –

like blood soaking into gauze.

iv
Reading old letters
on rainy days

makes you feel nostalgic.
You find the sight of a child

eating strawberries adorable,
but it infuriates you

when someone turns up unexpectedly
and stays talking for ages.

Reading your words,
the centuries, continents that divide us

seem to diminish, shrinking in size
like a fan snapped shut.

Your voice whispers to me
from the pages of your book:

soft as a pillow,
sharp as a paper cut.

On Entering the Eel Catcher's Workshop

A bell jangles above your head. In the gloom
it sounds like shattered glass.

Invisible fingers stroke your face;
you brush them aside, realise it's only

a spider's zip wire. As your eyes adjust,
shrouded shapes reveal themselves:

round shouldered barrels bound for London,
an outboard motor

that's stuttered itself into silence.
In the corner, an abandoned punting pole

puts down new roots. Unfinished willow traps
sprawl on the workbench, gaping mouths

already hungry. Beside them lies
a sly knife, its blade spotted with sap.

On the walls, former eel catchers
regard you sternly behind dust-grimed glass.

And right at the back of the shop,
glimpsed only for a second,

a look and a glittering smile
from the Eel Catcher's lovely daughter

before her slender form
dives deeper into the darkness.

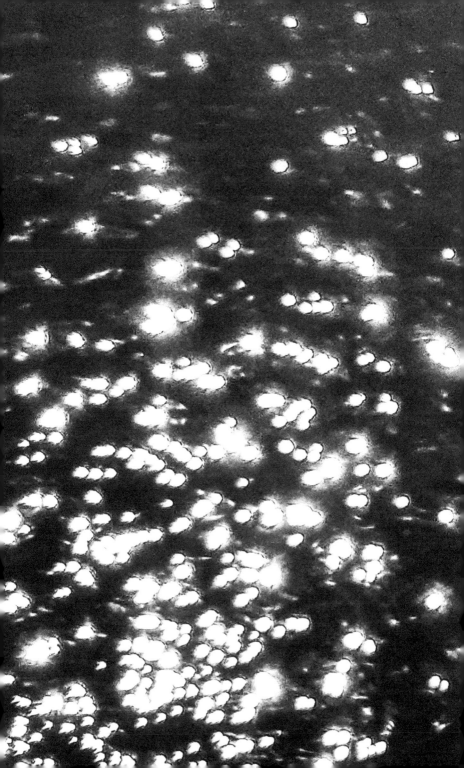

The Mermaid in the Dime Museum

As her village recedes to a distant speck,
she unpicks a loose stitch on the passenger seat. Her new boyfriend
turns, assures her of the wonderful life
waiting in the West. With her talent, she can easily
make it as a dancer. This will be her fortune.

> *A Japanese fisherman sits by the receding tide,*
> *sewing. Stitches smaller than rice grains*
> *seamlessly blend scales and fur.*
> *His finger tips trace the tail's sensuous curve.*
> *He smiles. This will be his fortune.*

Hair extensions; Brazilian; spray tan; acrylic nails.
She's worried about the cost, but her boyfriend doesn't hesitate,
hands his credit card over. As she leaves the salon
she sees Venus reflected in the glass:
new born, radiant, shawled in ocean mist.

> *The sum is more than five bolts of silk,*
> *but the Dutch merchant doesn't hesitate,*
> *pays the Japanese fisherman, wraps it in a shawl*
> *and carries it, tenderly as a newborn,*
> *up the gangplank.*

She wonders why her dance audition is in a hotel,
but her boyfriend tells her to shut the fuck up, stop asking questions.
The receptionist is indifferent; he's seen it all,
leads her through labyrinthine corridors to a plain white room.
The director looks her up and down; tells her to undress.

> *In an alley among whores, drunks and the stench of fish,*
> *the Dutch merchant strikes a bargain with an American captain,*
> *who has to sell his ship. Years later, broke, he sells the mermaid*
> *for a fraction of what he paid. But that's the way with sirens,*
> *bestowing fortune or grief as whim dictates.*

Bathed in his laptop's subaqueous glow,
a man wanders the internet's dark alleys, safe search off.

He finds a video of a girl with buoyant breasts
and hairless sex sprawled on the bed
of a white hotel room. He clicks.

> *The posters appear overnight: a genuine mermaid,*
> *caught off the shores of distant 'Feejee'. Crowds surge*
> *to the museum, pay their dime. The men go to catch a glimpse*
> *of milky skin, flowing hair, peeping nipples;*
> *the women to hear the songs she must surely sing.*

She dies several times a day; fakes so many little deaths
she's starting to feel a part of her has died inside.
By now she doesn't have to think: just curls her lips,
and, eyes glassy, looks at the wave-like patterns on the ceiling
while her co-star fills the red-pink shell of her sex.

> *Munching popcorn and cotton candy, the punters*
> *walk past waxworks of famous murderers, but still are not prepared*
> *for the sight of a blackened baby orangutan with a salmon tail.*
> *The Feejee Mermaid sprawls in its case,*
> *glass eyes reflecting all those drowned expressions,*
> *lips curled as though in laughter at some secret joke.*

Jam Jar

Trying to think of a gift
to give you for Valentine's Day,
because I know you aren't the type
who'd appreciate a card
with cuddling teddies on it,

or brittle flowers
from a petrol station,
or a bottle of something
that passes for pink champagne.
No, I think I will give you

a rinsed out jam jar. Trapped inside
is the sigh that escapes my lips
when, thinking of you,
my hand slips between my legs.
I had to get the lid on quickly

before, like a sly insect,
it darted out of reach.
To hear it, all you have to do
is hold the jar against your ear,
and slowly unscrew the lid.

Aaaaah, that's it.

Absinthe

Not possessing an ornate slotted spoon,
we dispense with the ceremony
of sugar cubes and iced water,

and drink the absinthe on the rocks.
We don't really need it –
we're already pissed, warm and giggly

after an evening of wine and reconciliations,
but you decide to indulge
my bohemian aspirations

and fill two tumblers with the eerie green.
We clink glasses
then watch the liquid cloud over.

The sugar crystals swirl,
snowflakes in a glass ornament.
The green struggles

a moment more,
then surrenders itself
to opacity and oblivion.

Three months later, I'm lying
on a hospital bed.
You're next to me, holding my hand.

A monitor is turned towards us.
Amid a grey, whispering blizzard
a new life is floating:

fluttering heartbeat, budding limbs.
Everything's fragile, yet perfectly formed,
like points on a snowflake.

White Rose in February

After Sophie Scholl

Such a fine, sunny day

The February sun shines bright, but it cannot warm. It's the kind
that blanches petals to translucence, but also blights.
In your cell you watch shadows creep, slicing the floor.

Being so short of days, February was always loathe
to lend you more. That's why you had so little time
in which to drop your leaflets

around the university. Now the small hand of the clock
is about to fall onto five. It's cut away
the four days since your arrest, the brief hours since your trial.

Such a fine, sunny day, and I have to go

The transcript of your interrogation must number
dozens of pages, like those left in your suitcase.
You knew the students would be spilling from their classes,

thought you had time to gift them a strange harvest, so sent
the pages fluttering like petals into the atrium below.
You didn't see the janitor slide back into the darkness.

I have to go

Now time has shrunk to the few steps it takes to cross
the prison yard. You place the stem of your neck through the lunette.
As it falls, the blade is bright and sharp as the February sun.

Чайка*

After Valentina Tereshkova

Even as a child you longed for space:
a bird-girl climbing the cherry trees
that edged the field of your existence,
free-falling through a nebula of blossom,
before crashing back down,
wearing your scabs like medals.

Years later you jumped from planes, trusting in
your parachute's silk and the Motherland
that built factories and put men in space.
In those weightless moments when your stomach
caught up with your body, you wondered if
Gagarin – your hero – had felt the same churning.

In '63 you clambered into
Vostok 6 and made your final checks,
safe within your helmet's halo. Meanwhile,
your comrades at the factory lifted their heads
above the machinery's prayer
and wondered at your absence.

Your call signal was Чайка, and like a seagull
circling a trawler you girdled the earth.
You felt nauseous, but the world felt your joy,
saw your smile shine through TVs grey squall,
your voice almost a squawk:
ya chaika. I am a seagull.

And as you re-entered earth's atmosphere,
parachute blossoming,
you drifted into myth,
transforming from a seagull into an *alkonost*:
a gold plumed bird-woman, bearing a message
from paradise to the waiting people below.

*Чайка – Chaika

The High Priestess of Gropekunte Lane

Opie Street, Norwich

Lovers – come close, no need to be afraid,
I only trade in secrets. I see you're on
a long weekend, sampling the languid time
between evening and night. Adventures wait
down every street, but indecision's sweet.
Perhaps this lane seems too respectable,

but like a doll whose skirt you lift
to show another face, Opie Street once wore
a different smile. Peel off the paint, chisel
away the Greek facades, strip layers till
you reach a time when cobbles were washed
with shit and piss. Hidden from the Castle's
narrowed, forbidding eyes, and where the ring

of the Cathedral's bells dissolves, my sisters
and I darkened the night like bats, our arms
spread wide, our skirts hitched high, awaiting the
straggle of men who nightly found themselves
reeled in by Gropekunte Lane's magnetic pull.
I knew them all: the childlike, moon-faced Fool

who swayed, gold coins dripping from his pockets,
supported by his friend, the quick fingered
Magician, whose touch misdirected me.
I heard the Hermit's crude unholy Creed,
panted in my ear. And though he was disguised,
I knew the Emperor by his long jaw.
At his request, I squeezed my hands around

the Hanged Man's throat, his little death making
him feel alive. The Devil came one night,
I'm sure. His skin was smooth, but sparks flew from
his heels as though he walked on flintlock hooves.
Women too, would come, begging advice
on how to keep love fresh, or herbs to drain

the life that swelled their white aprons like sails.
In darkness everyone's the same, shadows
blessing both rich and poor. Here, beneath
midnight's blind gaze I held my court: I was
the Queen of Cups, pouring favours on all
who came, the mighty and the damned. I saw
their hearts, grew holy on this power till I

became the High Priestess of Gropekunte Lane.
So as you pause, choosing which street to take,
consider this: you may appear to be
the image of ideal love – your arms
entwined, heads bowed in idle nothing talk,
but can your bond withstand a stroll along

this cobbled walk? I jest. Here you'll find
quaint restaurants, share cheesecake, see your face
shining and haloed in their eyes, but can
you ever know the fantasies that stir
inside their deepest and most secret core?
Gropekunte Lane once throbbed with longings such as these.
And though my sight is veiled by tattered years,

I've seen enough of humankind, know
desires don't change, despite the boulder roll
of time. So would you be prepared to do
the thing they whisper timidly, afraid
of what you'll think? And do you trust enough
to share the want that gnaws away at you?

The Eel Catcher Calls me Home

Those who escape the village with its ditches and damp
think they'll never return. I was the same.
Then you surfaced, gasping in my dreams.
In the morning I didn't stop to pack.

I'd thought the city would make me immune:
turn the village into a snow globe I could cast aside
when shaking it was no longer fun. But no glass dome
can contain these meadows or tireless winds

that make the clouds race. Here, one can wander
for miles, wander even further in one's mind.
Memories swirled then settled: your tales
of monstrous pike; the river full of eels

that swam into your traps of woven willow
and grew drowsy on the bitter bark; me on tiptoes
beside your workbench, watching your knife
glint in the gloom. Before my mind's dustsheets

could unveil it, I'd arrived at your workshop –
sunk to its knees. I had to stoop to enter.
The shadows gulped me. The stench of fish guts
was the same. I found you in the darkest corner,

a washed-up thing, thrashing to reach your true form.
Too much time spent in the realm of your prey,
you were a man-turned-eel, caught in a dark tangle
of sensations your mind couldn't fathom.

Like a willow I bent over you and wept,
watched my tears dome then trickle over your cracked lips.
Your tongue flicked. Before clouds filmed your eyes,
I saw a ray of recognition.

Tomorrow I'll arrange for a wicker casket.

Contacting Harry

After Bess Houdini

i

I had a magic of my own.
Not the smoke-and-glitter kind like yours,
but potent nonetheless.
My needle was my wand, stitching love
tight into the seams of your costumes.
On stage, I wove talismans about you
as I darted here, there,
pulling chains taut against your oiled chest.
Spotlit, my leotard shimmered, firebird bright,
but I made myself invisible,
so that all eyes were on you
as I lowered you, head first
                    into the tank.

ii

A Jack-in-the-box in reverse,
I could fold myself into a glass chest
just three feet square. I was your *sweetie* –
a slip of a girl. Perhaps that's why
I never mastered the trick
that comes naturally to most women.
I couldn't make blood spill like scarves
from the sleeve between my legs.
No child ever hung upside down
suspended in the watery chamber
                    of my womb.

iii

Like a faulty top hat
that can't stop birthing rabbits,
you filled our house with pets. But fur and feathers
weren't enough, so we dreamed ourselves a son –
Mayer – named for your father.
On tour you'd write me, ask how Mayer was getting on.
My pen was my wand now, sparks flying from the nib
as I conjured a scabby-kneed imp

with your curls and knack for escapades.
An indulgent mother, I gave him the best of everything.
But when I installed him in the White House,
he suddenly learnt the family trade,
slipped through the bars of my imagination
                              and vanished.

iv

After the blows to your abdomen,
you lingered in pain for nine days. You whispered
the code, confident that if anyone
could make contact from the afterlife, it would be you.
You escaped me on Hallowe'en – a showman to the end.
Two thousand came, followed your copper coffin's
slow progress to the Jewish Cemetery in Queens.
Although I should have been prepared,
I couldn't believe it, thought it was a new stunt –
that you'd broken your record for holding your breath,
and would leap out, the same as always
                              and take a bow.

v

Ten years on, and death's bars
hold you fast. Acceptance is still difficult.
That's why we're sitting in this circle,
as we do every Hallowe'en,
our hands fanned like dovetails.
I sit straight as a tuning fork. Yearning hums
through my body as I wait for your answering note.
You're there in the shadows, shackled and handcuffed,
struggling to get free. But the minutes,
heavy with realisation, tick by.
Oh darling, place your frozen lips on mine.
Let me slip you the key one last time.

The Baader-Meinhof Effect

Someone's coming through to me

on your Mother's side   someone called Cyril
      (the name means nothing to me)

There's a French connection and a royal connection too

            Look out for a white carnation

You don't like water much, do you?

That's because, in a past life

          you were on board the Titanic

     Look out for white feathers

I see you have an admirer   Do you ever hear voices?

Tell me about the maisonette – you felt unsettled

            as though you were being watched
      (this at least is true)

You're special like me – you have two guardian angels as well

       You're yet

     to meet your soulmate

          Your poems
are your angels   whispering

           When you acknowledge
your guardian angels, it will be as though

     a basket of feathers has been tipped from the sky

It's all bollocks, of course. But on my way home, my eye snags on a white streak. Further on, another feather, then another, each purer than the last. I think of the man on the internet who, on learning about the German terrorist group, kept hearing their name for days afterwards. But for a moment, I allow a thought, soft as a whisper: it's my guardian angels, laying a trail for me, guiding me home.

When Daedalus was my Lodger

I'd find the TV or soundsystem
dismantled on the coffee table, wires rearing
like the heads of the Hydra. He kept strange hours
and stranger company: bullish men and capricious boys.
Wax splats made starbursts on every surface
as he tested the melting temperature of candles.

> My husband muttered things about eviction.

He cooked for me when he couldn't pay the rent:
honey and sesame fritters, quince jellies,
but he always left the washing up.
He carved me knick knacks and thingmibobs,
but they flew away when I bent to look more closely.
We'd talk about the children that we'd lost.

> My husband suggested marriage counselling.

He'd wake at midday and wander the house,
unaware his robe wasn't properly tied
and that I could see everything: dark hair
curled tight as woodshavings. At night
I dreamt he turned me on his lathe,
my body taking shape beneath him.

> My husband handed me divorce papers.

An invisible thread guided me through
the labyrinth of his mind
and I knew that one day I'd open
his attic door and find him standing on the sill,
wings strapped to his back, the sun an aura around him.
I started collecting feathers, so that when the time came

> I could stand beside him, not caring
> if we soared
>
> or
>
> fell.

The Poet of Witch Countie –
A Tragedie in Five Acts

"When, however, one reads of a witch being ducked, of a woman possessed by devils, of a wise woman selling herbs... then I think we are on the track of a lost novelist, a suppressed poet"
Virginia Woolf, A Room of One's Own.

Act i

> *The summer is warm & damp.*
> *The bread is blacker than usual.*

Poems itch inside your head
but words are insects you cannot name
& you are a woman & therefore destined
to hold a needle & never a quill
& the low rhymes you drone as you sew
sound like spells.

Act ii

> *Carriage wheels rut the mud.*
> *The Witchfinder & his men are on their way.*

Stories swell inside you like dough.
You roll out pastry but dream of parchment.
You are a widow & reliant on alms
& your own small acts of kindness –
an apple & a kiss for your neighbour's son
must be a hex.
> *Exit the neighbour's son.*

Act iii

> *Fear's white head crowns like a mushroom;*
> *shapeshifts into rumour & breeds in the oozing alleys.*

You are ugly & therefore evil & therefore keep
an imp in your pocket
which you slipped through a hole

in the neighbour's door.
'Go & rock the cradle'
they say you said.

Act iv

> *The neighbour scratches your face*
> *till your blood clots her nails.*

Suddenly the pain she's felt for years is gone,
& the poems inside you, those familiar words
more dear to you than Bible verses
sour into curses as the Witchfinder's pricker
searches for the soft places
where you let the devil suck.

Act v

> *The villagers heckle beneath you;*
> *haggle over your scanty belongings.*

As the rope tightens about your throat,
you leave your body, rising higher, higher
above the hazy fields. Your eyes bulge
at imps only you can see.
Before your neck breaks like a great book snapping shut,
you dream of raining curses down
to blacken the rye & make it wither
like words dying on a tongue.

The Poacher's Daughter

What's that stench of guts and slaughter?
Must be the Poacher's mad March daughter.

My mother was witchy-beautiful,
but even her looks and the pouches of herbs
she slipped in his pockets couldn't snare my father –
he left while I still leapt and boxed inside her.

Bad luck
for a pregnant woman to see a hare
mother says
one crossed her path the moonlit night
she took the shortcut home.
Frozen in those headlamp eyes
something was transferred.

They should've sunk the runt in ditch water.
Here comes the Poacher's hare-lipped daughter.

The midwife made the sign of the cross
when she pulled me, feet first, downed with coarse fur
from the sprung trap between my mother's legs –
a hare's kiss planted on my upper lip.
The other children laugh. Throw stones,
whispers hissing like wind in long grass.
I smell their fear, sour as crushed piss-pipes.

Turn away. Show her no quarter.
Run from the Poacher's long-lugged daughter.

I met my father once, in a field,
under the speckled shell of the Egg Moon.
Something snagged my ankle and I stumbled.
I lay, twitching; watched him raise his rifle, take aim.
His eyes widened, headlamp-large as I shrugged off my coat.
Understanding flowed between us like a breeze
before I freed myself and staggered away.

Sometimes we pass each other in the street.
He keeps his gaze ahead, the knives and charms on his belt
jangling in time to his stride.
It's not till he thinks I'm gone
that I see him touch his lucky paw.

She's the Poacher's secret torture:
his stump-footed, limping daughter.

The Summerlands
for N.F.

Once we scratched pentagrams into dirt
and hung black ribbons from branches
to make a sacred grove. When the other kids
turned up, hunters on their BMXs,
you were already gone,
swift as a doe.

Later we lay on your bed, plucking cards
from your tarot pack. You always got the High Priestess.
Our talk was magic. We sniggered at the
sympathetic kind. You told me about the Summerlands –
where witches are reborn. Then you traced
a future in my palm, arousing a strange alchemy.

Years later, I find you naked, crouched
in a dark corner of the web, a skull between your legs.
Your smile hints at things I don't know the name for,
but your eyes are somewhere else.

So if I should think of you,
let it not be as you are,
but as you were. Better still,
let me think of you
as you might like to be:
standing in our sacred grove

on a simmering midsummer night. The birds
awaken as you kneel down, shrug off
your human shape. The moon spots your flanks with white,
makes your now black eyes shine once more.
Hesitant on legs thin as hazel wands, you trot,

gaining speed as you make for where
moonlight slants a narrow door.
You leap; kick your hind legs out:
the last part of you
to leave this world.

Omens

'She [Boudica] employed a species of divination, letting a hare escape from the fold of her dress; and since it ran on what they considered the auspicious side, the whole multitude shouted with pleasure.'
Dio Cassius

And when I was cut down from the whipping post,
limp and bloody, welts criss-crossing my back
like the branches of a bonfire,
I knew how I would exact my vengeance.

When I was healed
                    I trapped a hare;
placed its struggling body at my feet

                              then let it go.

In its mad, zig-zagging course
I saw my enemies scattering,
as though from burning huts.

My men and I rode south, to Camulodunum,
where the townsfolk cowered in the temple.
                            I lit the torch

          heard them shrill like pigs.

          Then on to Londinium

the scent of death trailing behind like a cloak.

Each town was the same:
blackened bodies on smouldering stubble.
My blade, lightning swift, struck
those the flames had not taken.
Above, smoke swirled like the ghosts of crows.

My army grew. I was sure
my name must echo in the Emperor's ears.

I searched for signs,
                              swore at the sight
of a calf born breech, wondered at
the stocking of a shed snakeskin.

I turned my back on battlefields,
haunted the cool shadows of oak groves,
prayed for a vision.

But when the trance took me,
                              what I saw
was not myself
                    red hair streaming
igniting the wind,

but a hare
            trying to outrun

the iron tip of an airborne arrow.

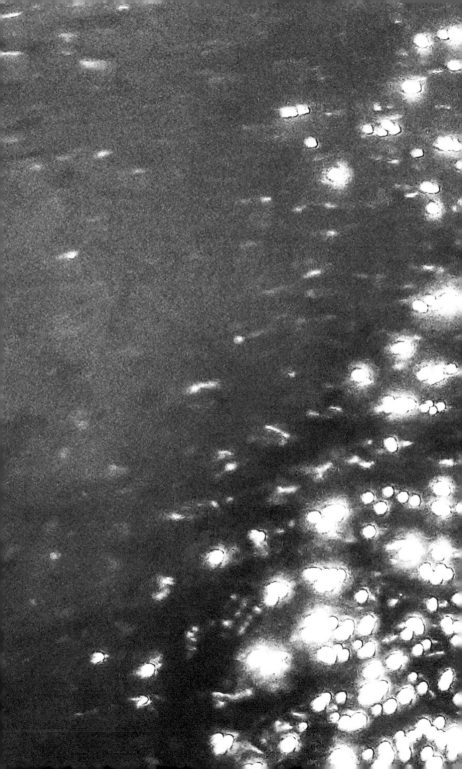

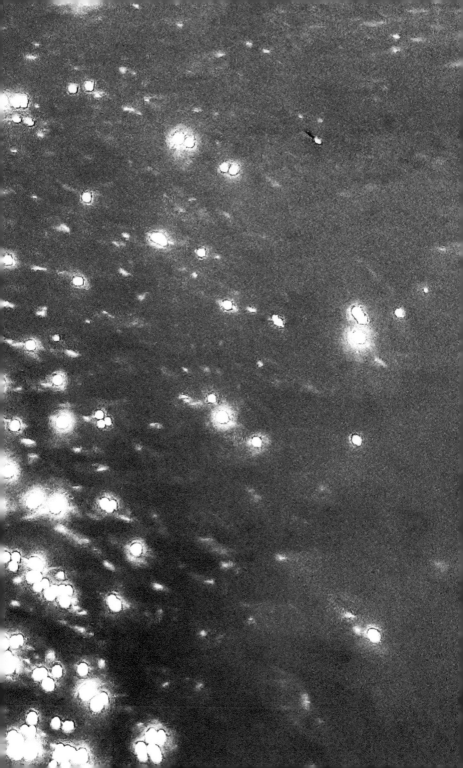

The Last Lady Eel Catcher

After Liz Berry

I'm the last lady eel catcher,
know the waterways
as well as the veins in my wrist,

spend my days
going up and down the river
like a bead sliding on a string.

At sunset I set
my traps of woven willow,
return before dawn's grey yawn

has swallowed the last stars.
I leave the empty ones where they are,
tip the full ones into my tank,

watch liquid silver
flash past my fingers.
When the sun

slices open the sky,
I punt to the village
to sell my squirming catch.

Once a year I put on my best clothes,
kneel before the parchment-skinned Bishop
to pay my slippery tax.

He peers into the creel,
sees the writhing silken bodies,
gasps as though he's seen a miracle.

Treasure

St. Mary the Virgin, Wissington, Suffolk

If I took you to see the dragon in the church
it would be at the end of summer,
on a day that's scorched and still,
when the Stour flows heavy as molten lead.

We'll pass nonplussed cows, clamber over
stiles, balance on narrow bridges.
Stubble will claw our ankles and midges
will tapestry the rippling air.

There'll be no need for talk; half-bewitched,
we'll follow the trail of a half-forgotten tale
till we spy the round tower nesting in the trees.
Pushing the heavy doors, you'll see it at once:

vivid against the pallid walls, its head looking back,
as though in defiance at some foolhardy knight,
its tail ending with a flourish. You'll think
of the restorers – how their fingers must have burned

as layers of whitewash and Puritan shame
were stripped away till the dragon reared up –
still smouldering – the colour of
baked earth, dried blood, passion.

Leaving you to marvel, I'll watch dust dance
in shafts of jewelled light, imagine they're
all the prayers this church has ever heard.
A longing will be kindled and my own prayer

will rise like smoke: *Please let me feel your breath,
fierce on my face once more. Burn for me.
Let me lie beneath you, glittering.
Let me be your treasure, jealously guarded.*

The Choirmaster's Bees

My sermon on God's Plan remains unwritten.
Every time I attempt it, the words become little black legs

scrambling over the page, and my thoughts
crawl over each other. Today I wondered

if starlings carry God's Plan when they rise
in protestation at the cathedral bells.

Is God's Plan coiled tight within the spiral
on a snail's back? I ponder this

between services as I wind up and down the staircase.
I stand in the organ loft, watching pilgrims

mill beneath me. Beyond, the Choirmaster
calls his choristers to order. He is an affable man,

has hewn smooth sounds from the rough stone
of the local boys' voices, but his insistence

on keeping bees in our shared study
is testing me. Three frames stand upright

on my shelves. Honey drips down the embossed spines,
pools on my papers. Is God's Plan in the nectar

bees suck from the herbs in the cloister garden? Is it
packed into the perfect hexagons of their combs?

The Choirmaster taps his baton. The pilgrims become still.
Their muted humming fades away.

The same pure note rises from each boy's mouth.
The cathedral fills with sweetness.

Tenancy

There was no clause stating I'd have to share with ghosts –
those who were just passing through,
alighting like bees on a bush

before going on their way.
Mostly they don't bother me,
but sometimes they'll leave a reminder:

a tarnished teaspoon at the back of a drawer;
on the flower bed, a toy soldier fallen in action.
Lives wiped away

like mould that blooms on a window frame,
or painted over with thick magnolia strokes.
Existences masked, but not erased,

lingering like the must of damp,
seeping into layers of plaster and brick.
Sometimes I think I can hear them:

in the ripple of breath behind the curtains;
in the walls that hum like a hive
before a frame's removed.

Potential

It's a wedding of sorts, but with no vows or candles
to lend dignity to the transaction –
just me and a man with grease-blackened fingers.
I hand him my ring. The goldsmith rotates it,
peering through an eyeglass.
Hallmark found, he clatters it onto digital scales.
The numbers arabesque then settle:
a gram for every year of marriage.
A deal is struck; papers signed. The ring crowns
the bald pate of his thumb as he counts
bright amethyst and amber notes into my palm.
They crackle with potential
as I fold them into my purse.

Leaving, I think how
it will be tossed into a crucible
with scraps from other failed relationships.
It will weep scalding tears
as the goldsmith's hammer rings,
before it cools to an O –
an echo of the shape it held before.
But like a bulb that leaves a trace
even when one's eyes are closed,
I'll imagine the ring when it glowed brightest:
how it burnt the goldsmith's retinas,
pulsed and shimmered
with all the things it could become.

The Eel Catcher Dreams of Horses

Once, people believed gods dwelt here:
the waterways that fringe the fens.
They made offerings

of brooches, bronze daggers, embroidered bridles –
placed them at the invisible thresholds
where land and water meld. These days

the only river gods are eels, my votives
bits of roadkill to lure them inside my traps.
Vagrant spirits, eels slip in and out

of different realms, can sidle over
dew-tipped grass, crawl up the throats of estuaries,
where their gills taste the fizz of brine.

In my sleep I swim with them to their spawning ground,
the Sargasso Sea, where kelp weaves snares
for ships, makes men go mad with thirst.

Here Spanish *marineros* threw horses overboard –
sacrifices to the Virgin, or whatever deities
would listen to their rasping prayers.

Then my dreams are filled with whinnies,
thrashing necks, fetlocks snapped like matches,
and below, the eels, circling, circling.

Acknowledgements

Many thanks to the editors of the following anthologies, newspapers and zines where these poems first appeared: *Best of British* ('Omens'); *Hallelujah for 50ft Women* ('The Mermaid in the Dime Museum'); *In Transit* ('Chaika'); *Ornith-ology,* ('The Garden of Intelligence'); *Small Word* ('Absinthe'); *The New European* ('White Rose in February'); *The Stare's Nest* ('Tenancy'); and *Under the Radar* ('Potential').

'Lessons for an Apprentice Eel Catcher' won the 2015 Manchester Cathedral Poetry prize. A version of 'The Postman and the Swans' won the 2013 New Writer prize for best single poem. 'The Last Lady Eel Catcher' came second in the 2015 Suffolk Poetry Society's George Crabbe Memorial Prize, and 'Treasure' was commended. 'The Eel Catcher Dreams of Horses' was placed third in the 2014 Essex Poetry Festival Open Poetry Competition, and 'On Entering the Eel Catcher's Workshop' was highly commended in 2012. 'Becoming Sei' was highly commended in the 2013 Poetry London prize. 'Contacting Harry' and 'The Poacher's Daughter' were both commended in the *Mslexia* Women's Poetry Competition in 2015 and 2016 respectively.

Lightning Source UK Ltd.
Milton Keynes UK
UKHW041912100919
349541UK00001B/41/P

9 780993 125959